BIG-NOTE PIANO

Halloween Favorites

ISBN 978-1-4584-1572-1

HAL•LEONARD®
CORPORATION

7777 W. BLUEMOUND RD. P.O. BOX 13819 MILWAUKEE, WI 53213

Visit Hal Leonard Online at
www.halleonard.com

ADDAMS FAMILY THEME

Theme from the TV Show and Movie

Music and Lyrics by
VIC MIZZY

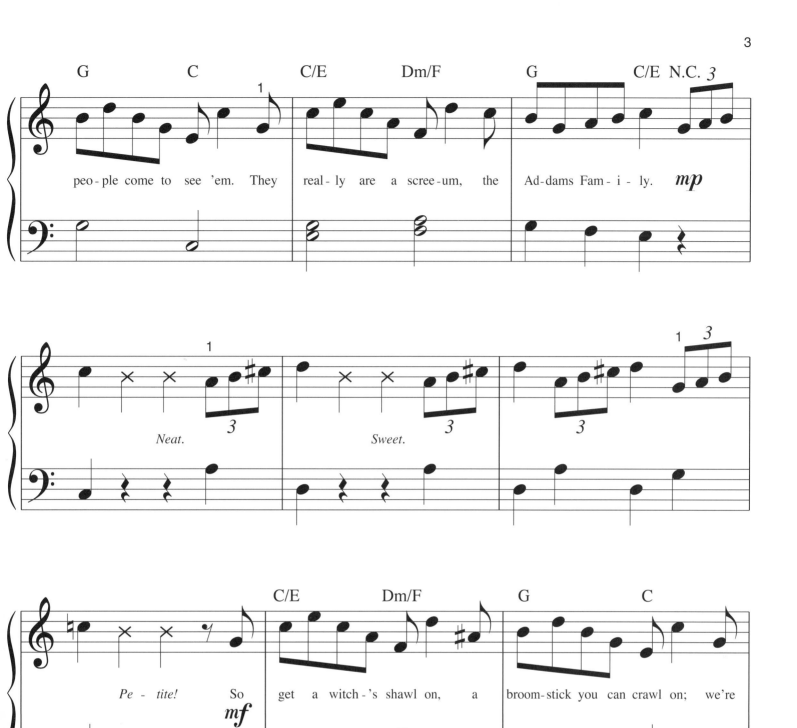

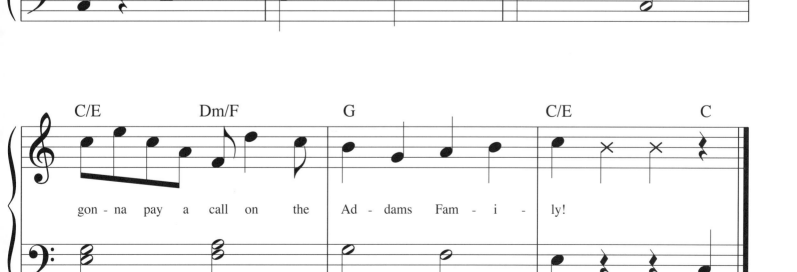

8vb

CASPER THE FRIENDLY GHOST

from the Paramount Cartoon

Words by MACK DAVID
Music by JERRY LIVINGSTON

With spirit

mf

Cas - per the friend - ly ghost, the friend - li - est ghost you know. Though grown - ups might look at him with fright, the chil - dren all love him so. Cas - per the

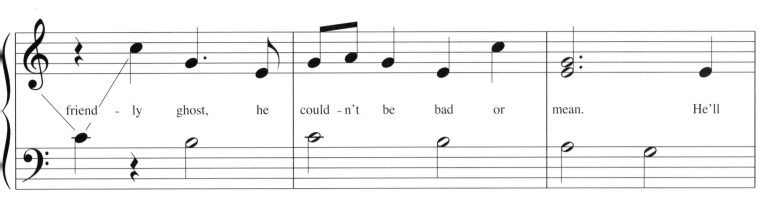

friend - ly ghost, he could -n't be bad or mean. He'll

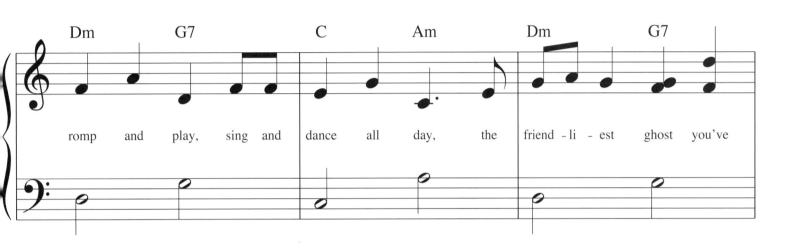

romp and play, sing and dance all day, the friend -li - est ghost you've

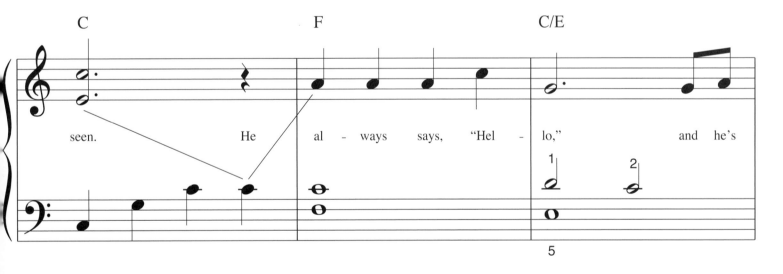

seen. He al - ways says, "Hel - lo," and he's

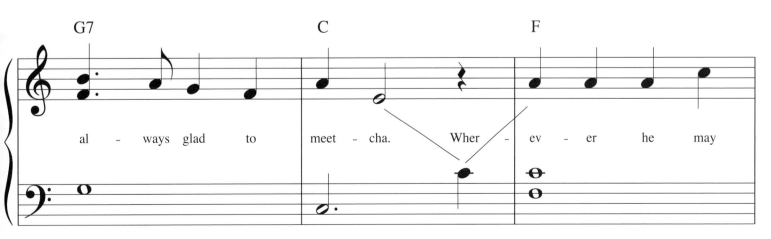

al - ways glad to meet - cha. Wher - ev - er he may

FUNERAL MARCH OF A MARIONETTE

featured in the Television Series ALFRED HITCHCOCK PRESENTS

By CHARLES GOUNOD

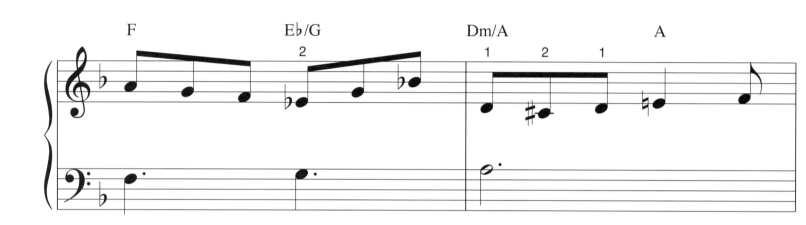

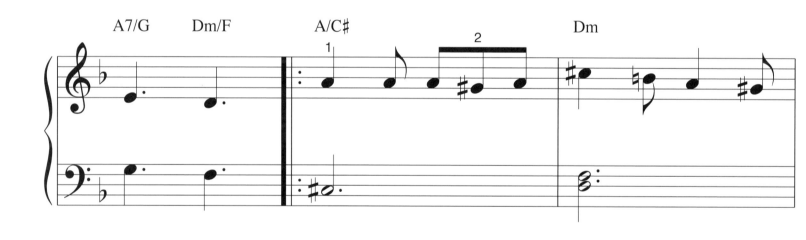

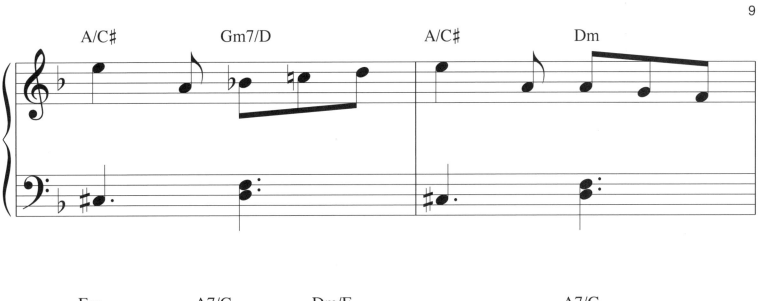

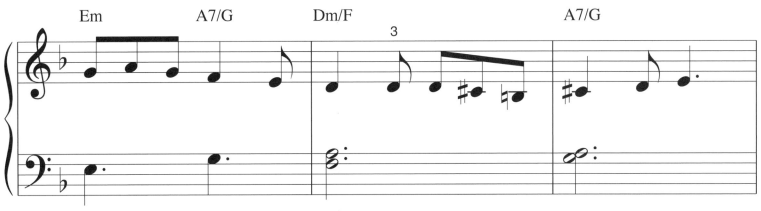

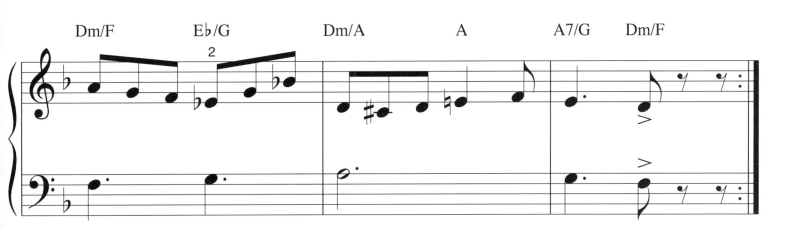

FUNERAL MARCH
from PIANO SONATA IN B-FLAT MINOR, OP. 35

By FRYDERYK CHOPIN

THEME FROM "JAWS"

from the Universal Picture JAWS

By JOHN WILLIAMS

Very steady and threatening

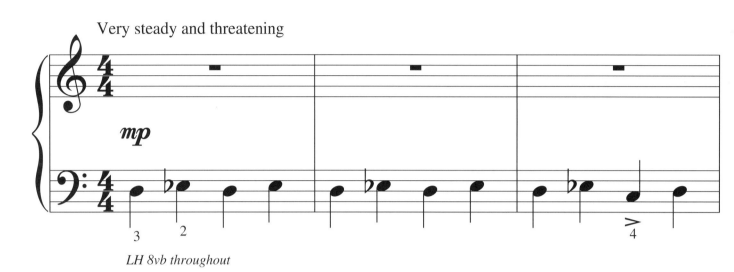

LH 8vb throughout

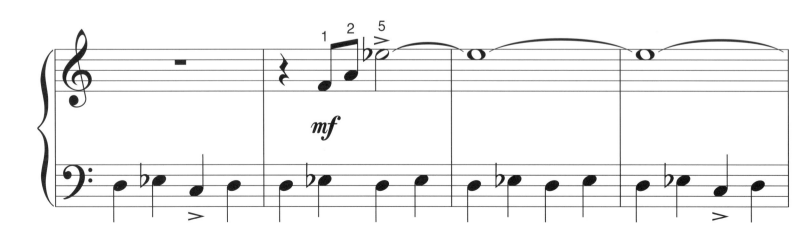

LITTLE SHOP OF HORRORS
from the Stage Production LITTLE SHOP OF HORRORS

Words by HOWARD ASHMAN
Music by ALAN MENKEN

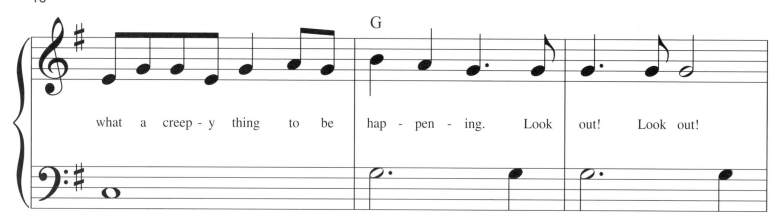

what a creep-y thing to be hap-pen-ing. Look out! Look out!

Shang - a - lang, feel the sturm and drang in the air.

Yeah, yeah, yeah. Sha - la - la, stop right where you are. Don't-cha

move a thing. You bet - ter, you bet - ter,

tell - in' you, you bet - ter   tell your ma - ma   some-thing's gon - na get   her.

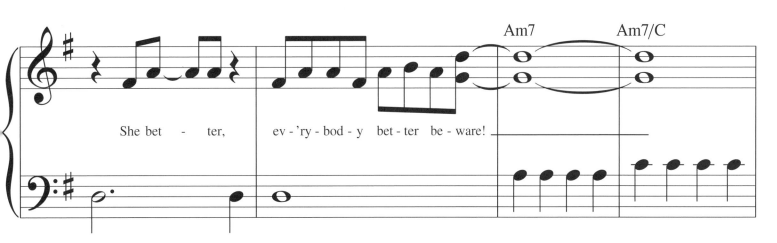

She bet - ter,   ev - 'ry - bod - y bet - ter be - ware!

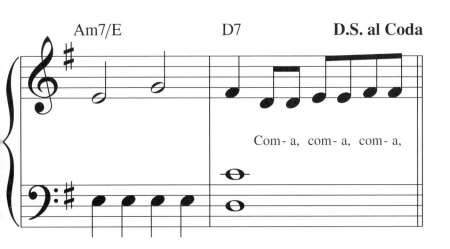

Am7/E   D7   **D.S. al Coda**   **CODA**   G   Am

Com - a, com - a, com - a,   No,   oh,   oh,

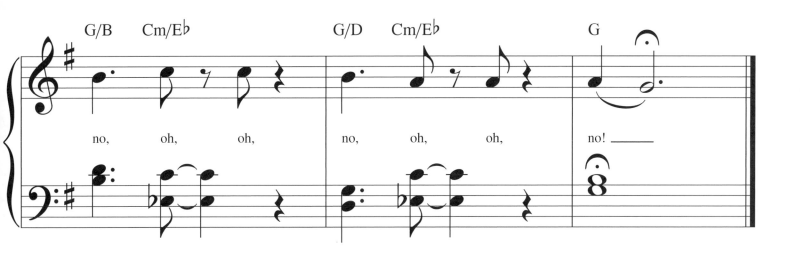

G/B   Cm/E♭   G/D   Cm/E♭   G

no,   oh,   oh,   no,   oh,   oh,   no! _____

MONSTER MASH

Words and Music by BOBBY PICKETT
and LEONARD CAPIZZI

Medium Rock

(Spoken:)
1. *I was working in the lab late one night,*
2. *laboratory in the*
3.-6. *(See additional lyrics)*

when my eyes beheld an eerie sight, for
castle east, to the master bedroom where the

19

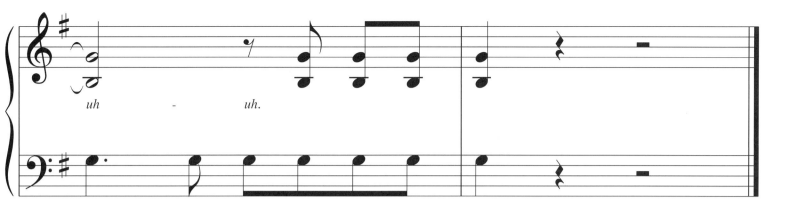

uh - uh.

Additional Lyrics

3. *The zombies were having fun,*
   The party had just begun,
   The guests included Wolf-man,
   Dracula, and his son.
   Chorus

4. *The scene was rockin'; all were digging the sounds,*
   Igor on chains, backed by his baying hounds.
   The coffin-bangers were about to arrive
   With their vocal group "The Crypt-Kicker Five."
   Chorus

5. *Out from his coffin, Drac's voice did ring;*
   Seems he was troubled by just one thing.
   He opened the lid and shook his fist,
   And said, "Whatever happened to my Transylvanian twist?"
   Chorus

6. *Now everything's cool, Drac's a part of the band*
   And my monster mash is the hit of the land.
   For you, the living, this mash was meant too,
   When you get to my door, tell them Boris sent you.
   Chorus

THE MUNSTERS THEME
from the Television Series

By JACK MARSHALL

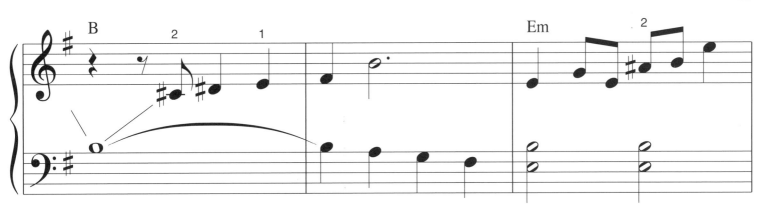

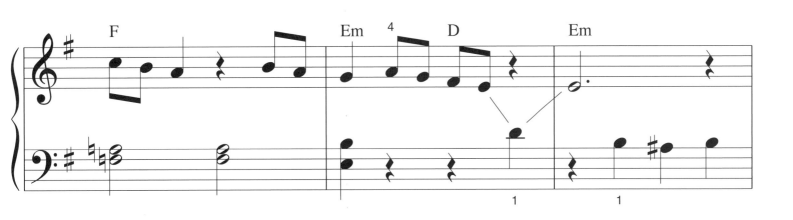

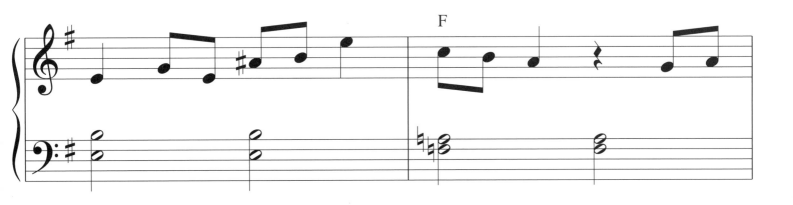

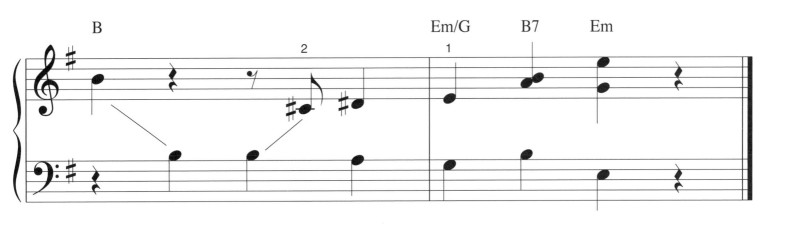

THE PHANTOM OF THE OPERA
from THE PHANTOM OF THE OPERA

Music by ANDREW LLOYD WEBBER
Lyrics by CHARLES HART
Additional Lyrics by RICHARD STILGOE
and MIKE BATT

Moderately fast

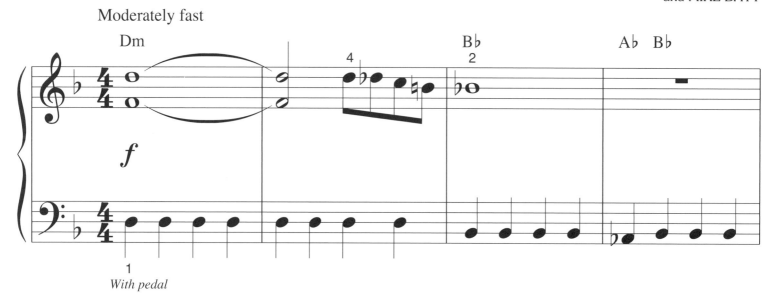

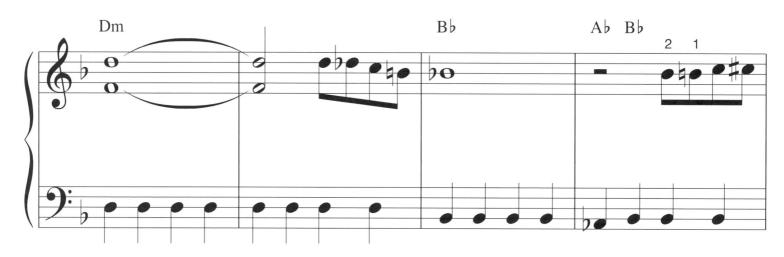

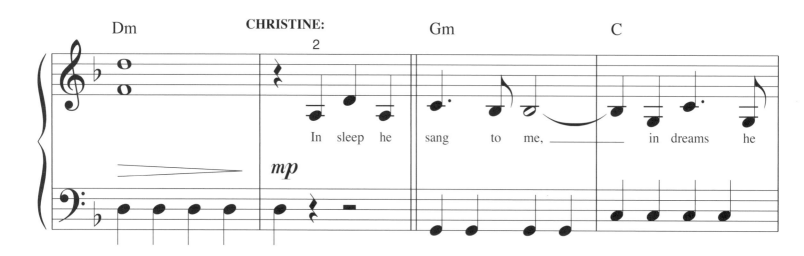

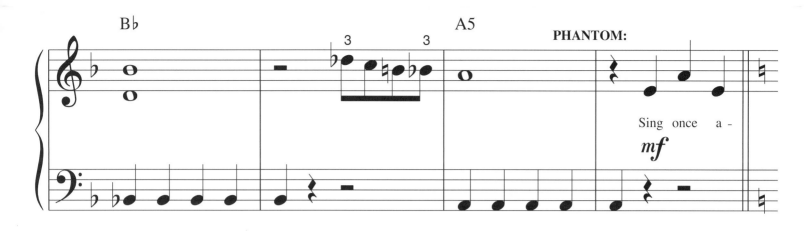

PHANTOM:

Sing once a-
mf

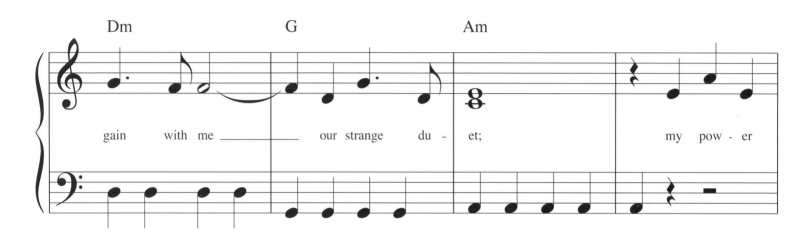

gain with me _____ our strange du - et; my pow - er

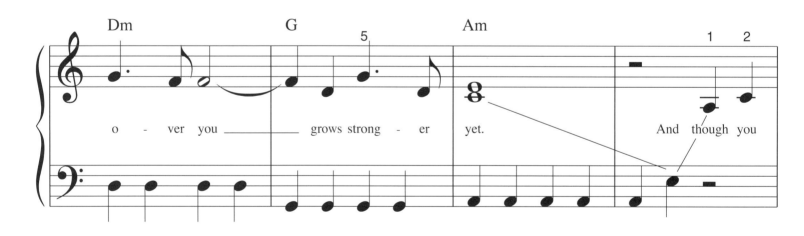

o - ver you _____ grows strong - er yet. And though you

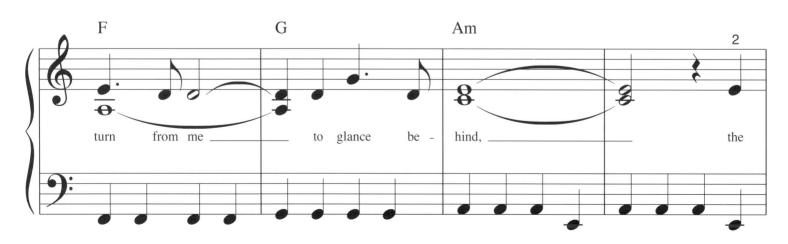

turn from me _____ to glance be - hind, _____ the

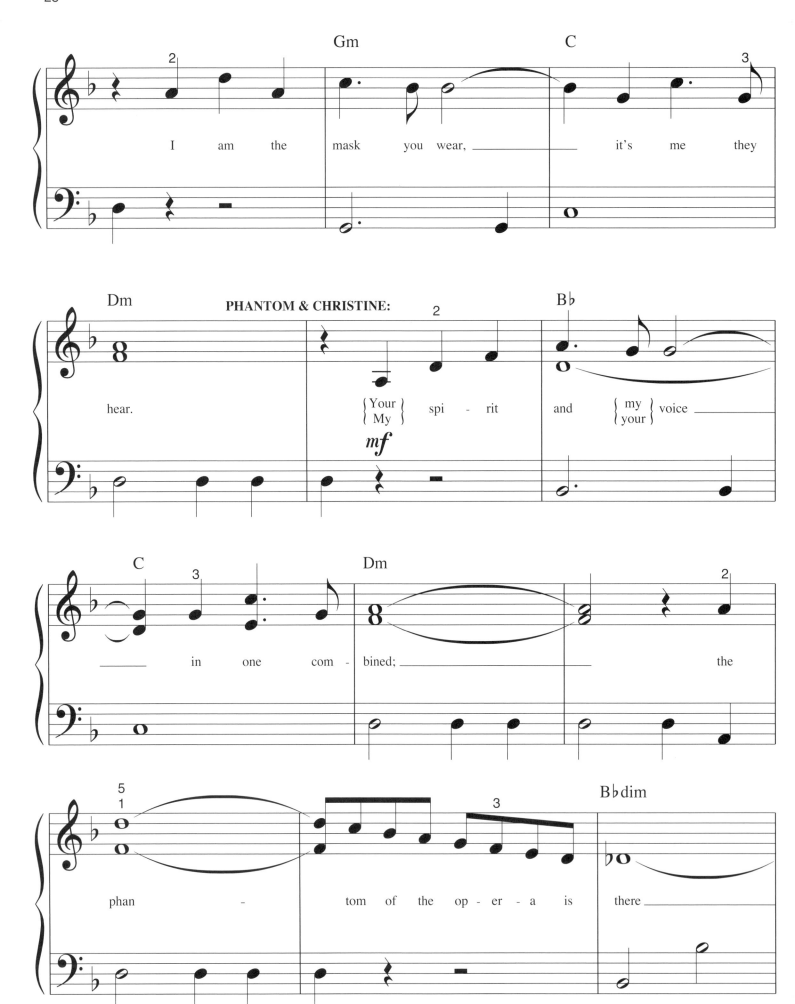

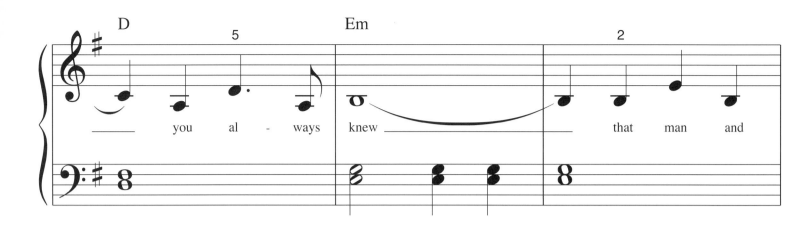

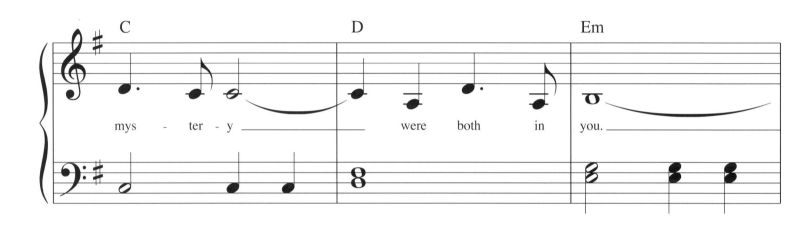

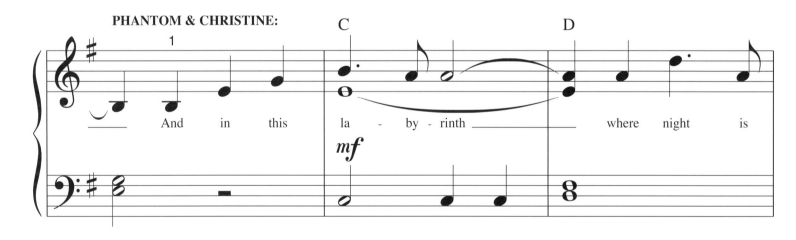

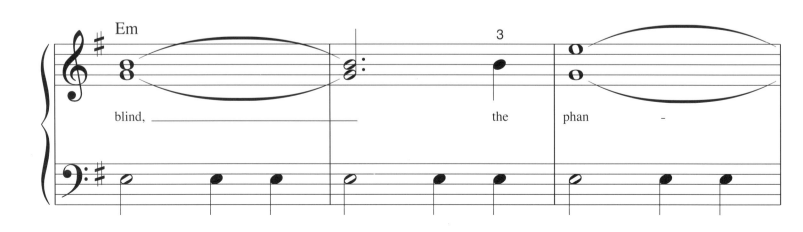

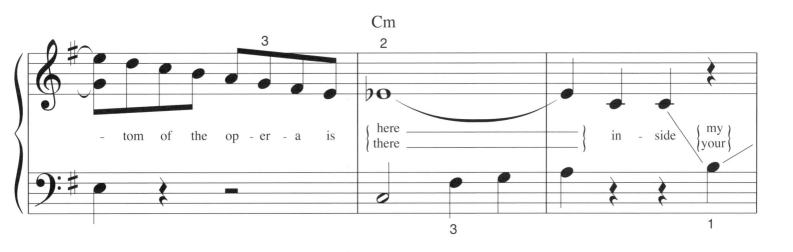

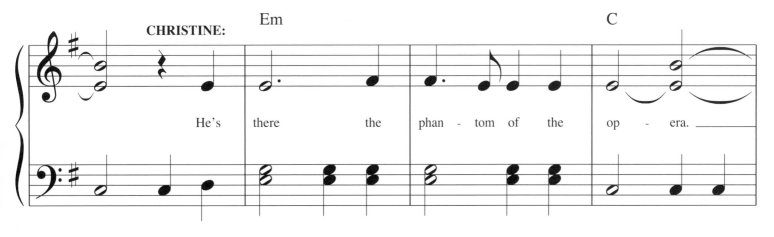

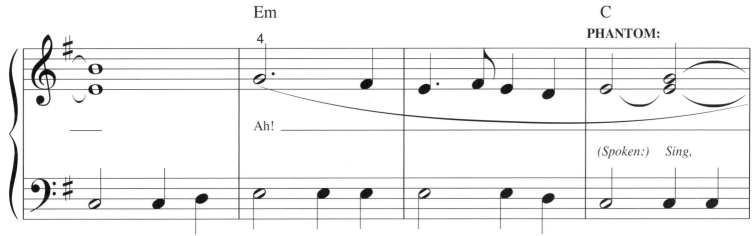

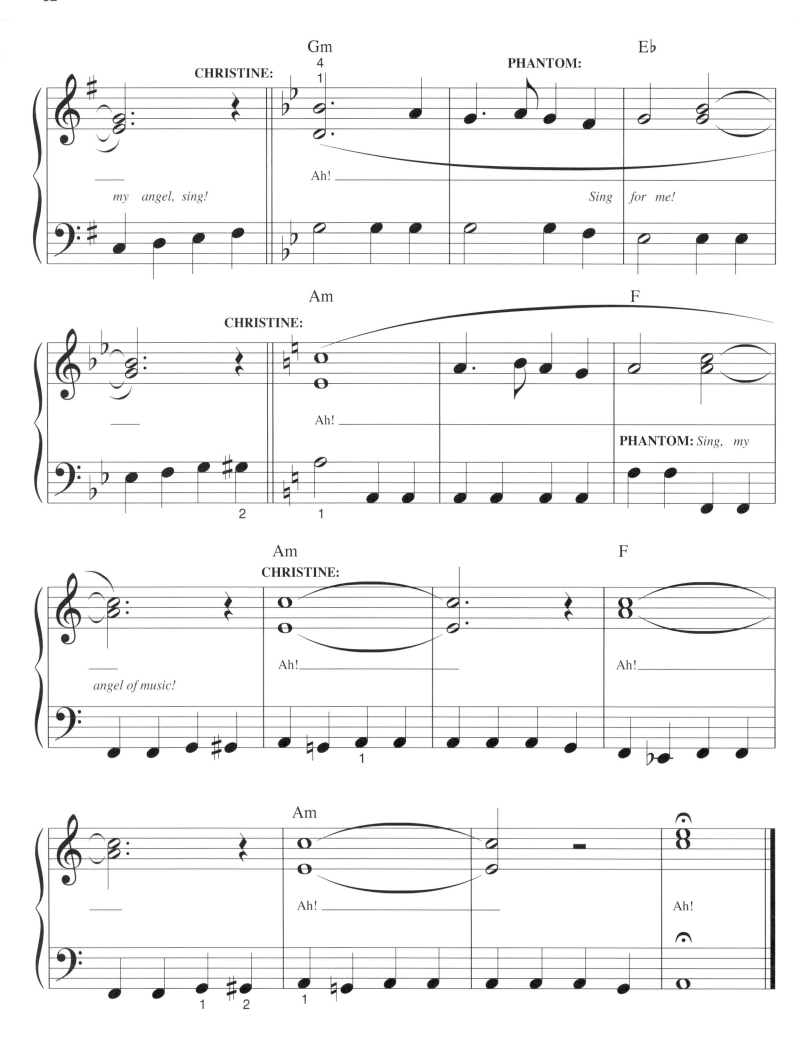

THE SORCERER'S APPRENTICE

from FANTASIA

By PAUL DUKAS

Moderately fast

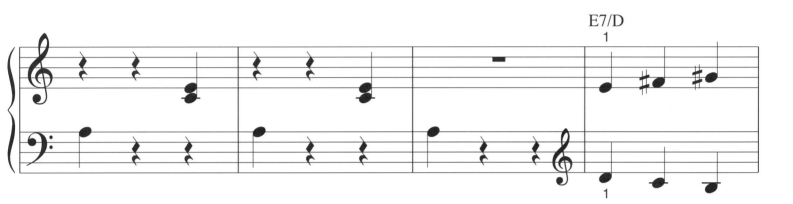

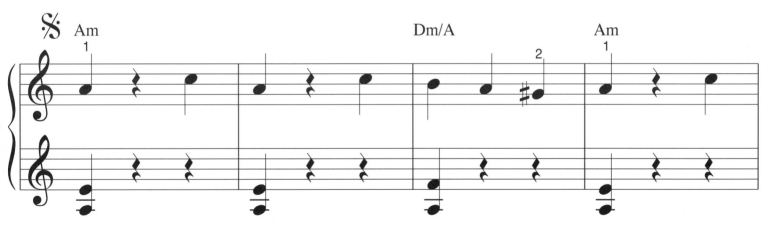

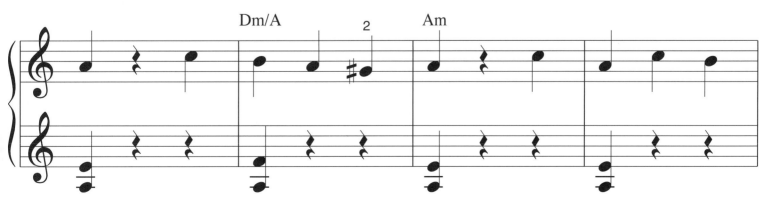

PSYCHO
(Prelude)
Theme from the Paramount Picture PSYCHO

Music by
BERNARD HERRMANN

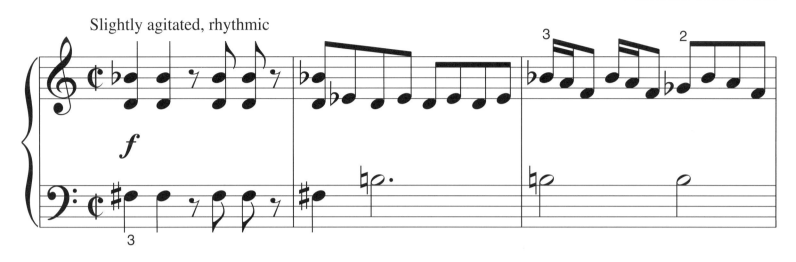

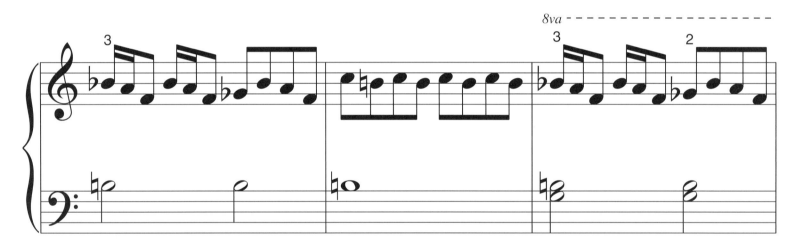

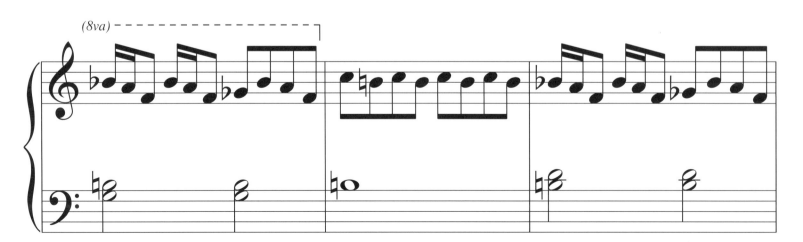

PURPLE PEOPLE EATER

Words and Music by
SHEB WOOLEY

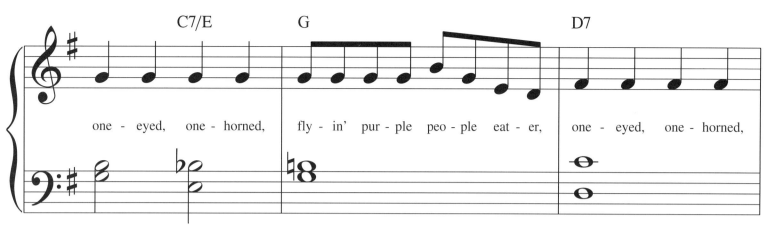

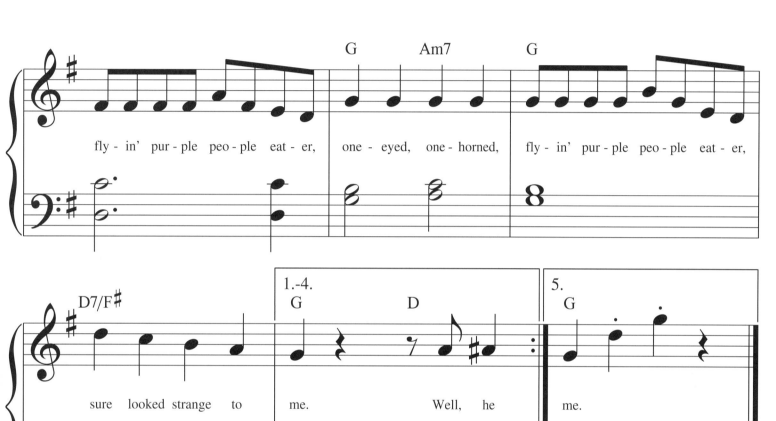

Additional Lyrics

2. Well, he came down to earth and he lit in a tree.
   I said, "Mister purple people eater, don't eat me."
   I heard him say in a voice so gruff,
   "I wouldn't eat you 'cause you're so tough."

   Well, bless my soul, rock 'n' roll, flyin' purple people eater,
   Pigeontoed, undergrowed, flyin' purple people eater,
   He wears short shorts, friendly little people eater.
   What a sight to see.

3. I said, "Mister purple people eater, what's your line?"
   He said, "Eatin' purple people, and it sure is fine,
   But that's not the reason that I came to land,
   I wanna get a job in a rock and roll band."
   It was a...

4. And then he swung from the tree and he lit on the ground,
   And he started to rock, a-really rockin' around.
   It was a crazy ditty with a swingin' tune,
   Sing a bob bapa lap a loom bam boom.
   It was a...

5. Well, he went on his way and then what-a you know,
   I saw him last night on a TV show,
   He was blowin' it out, really knockin' 'em dead,
   Playin' rock 'n' roll music through the horn in his head.
   It was a...

THIS IS HALLOWEEN
from Tim Burton's THE NIGHTMARE BEFORE CHRISTMAS

Music and Lyrics by
DANNY ELFMAN

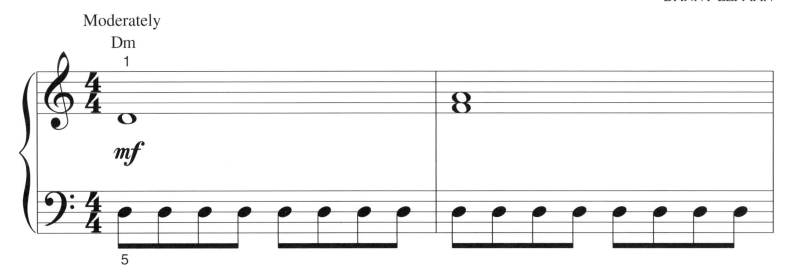

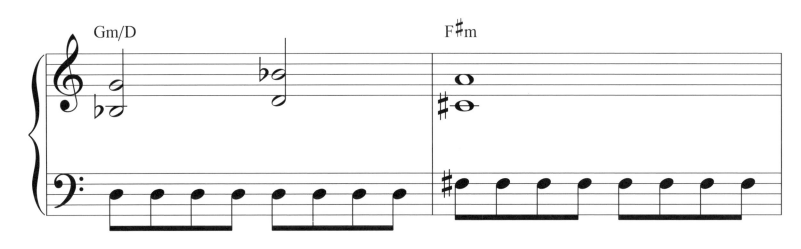

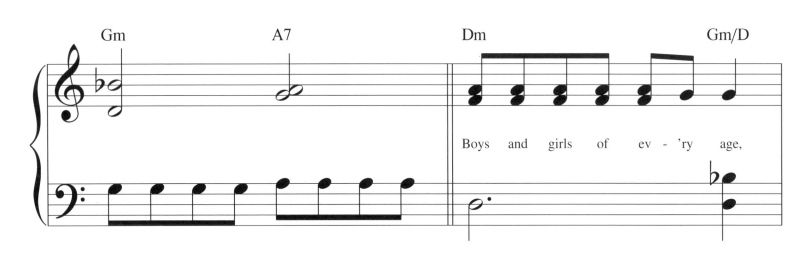

Boys and girls of ev-'ry age,

THRILLER

Words and Music by
ROD TEMPERTON

Moderately bright

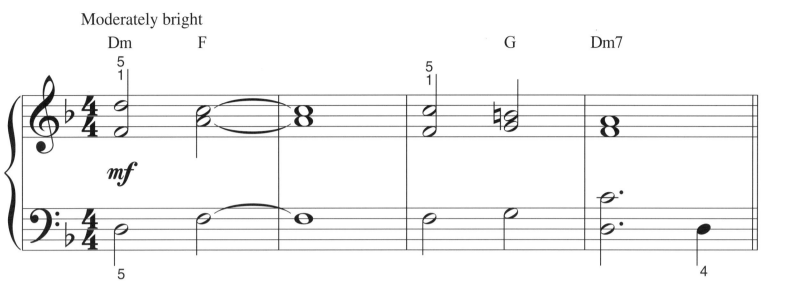

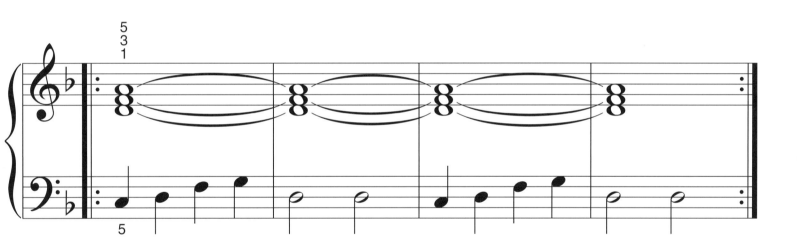

It's close to mid - night _____ and
You hear the door slam _____ and
They're out to get you. _____ There's

2. killer
thrill - er to - night. ____

Night crea - tures call and the dead start to walk in their

mas - quer - ade. ____

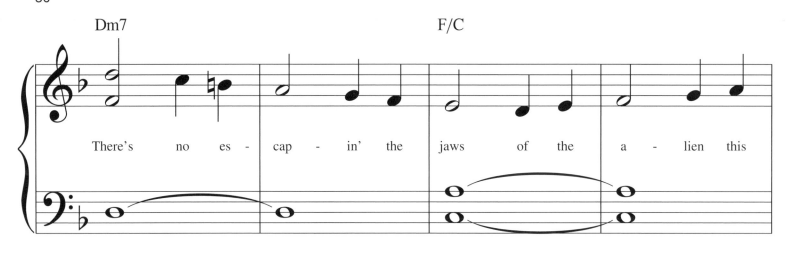

There's no es - cap - in' the jaws of the a - lien this

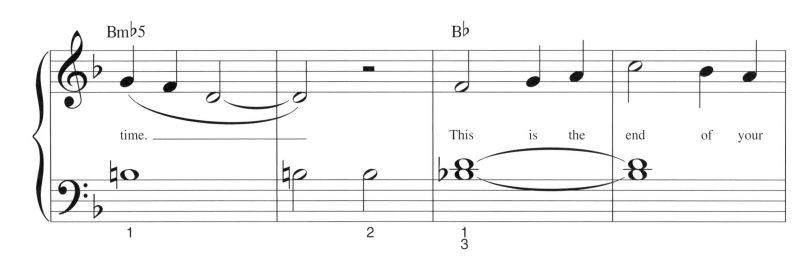

time. This is the end of your

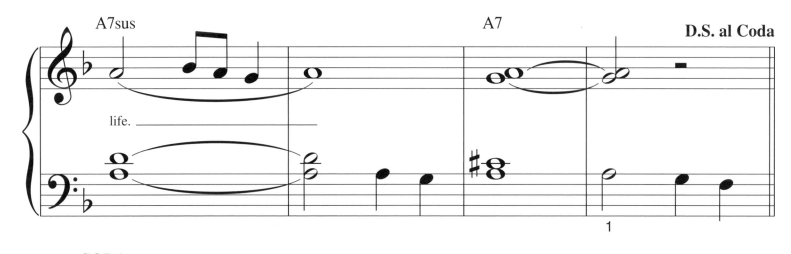

life.

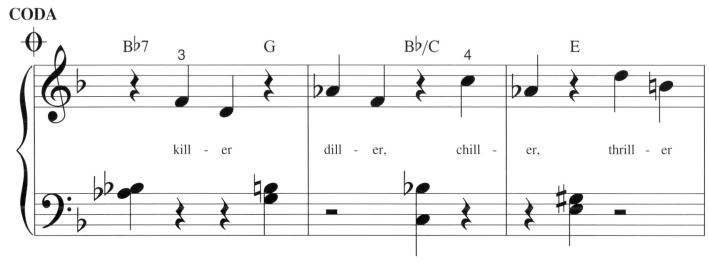

kill - er dill - er, chill - er, thrill - er

TUBULAR BELLS
Theme from THE EXORCIST

By MIKE OLDFIELD

Steadily

With pedal

THEME FROM THE X-FILES

from the Twentieth Century Fox Television Series THE X-FILES

By MARK SNOW

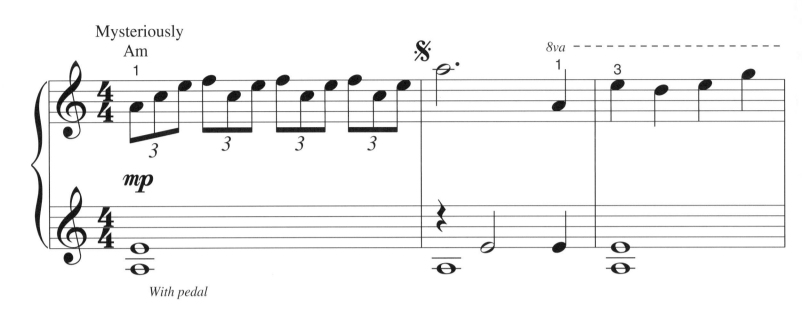

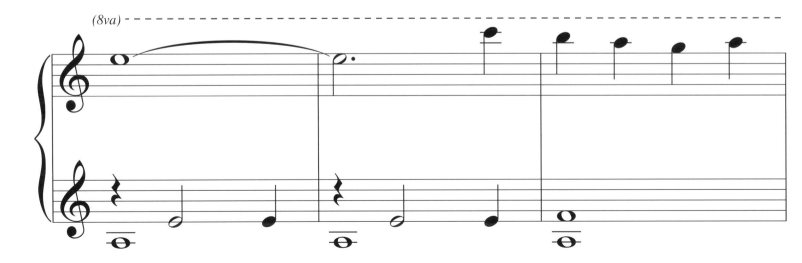

To Coda ⊕

TWILIGHT ZONE MAIN TITLE

from the Television Series

By MAURIUS CONSTANT

Mysteriously, with motion